W9-AUX-226

The Cornflake King

W. K. Kellogg and His Amazing Cereal

Edwin Brit Wyckoff

Enslow Elementary

an imprint of

Enslow Publishers, Inc.

40 Industrial Road
Box 398
Berkeley Heights, NJ 07922
USA

http://www.enslow.com

Content Adviser
Adam Shapiro
Education Communications Consultant

Series Literacy Consultant
Allan A. De Fina, Ph.D.
Dean, College of Education and Professor of Literacy Education
New Jersey City University
Past President of the New Jersey Reading Association

Enslow Elementary, an imprint of Enslow Publishers, Inc.

Enslow Elementary® is a registered trademark of Enslow Publishers, Inc.

Library of Congress Cataloging-in-Publication Data

Wyckoff, Edwin Brit.
    The cornflake king : W.K. Kellogg and his amazing cereal / Edwin Brit Wyckoff.
        p. cm. — (Genius at work! Great inventor biographies)
    Includes bibliographical references and index.
    Summary: "Readers will learn about W. K. Kellogg, and the creation of cornflakes"—Provided by publisher.
    ISBN-13: 978-0-7660-3448-8
    ISBN-10: 0-7660-3448-8
    1. Kellogg, W. K. (Will Keith), 1860-1951—Juvenile literature. 2. Industrialists—United States—Biography—Juvenile
literature. 3. Philanthropists—United States—Biography—Juvenile literature. 4. Kellogg Company—History—Juvenile
literature. 5. Cereal products industry—United States—History—Juvenile literature. 6. W.K. Kellogg Foundation—History—
Juvenile literature. I. Title.
    HD9056.U6K458 2010
    338.7'664756092—dc22
    [B]

                                    2009032848

Printed in the United States of America

042010 Lake Book Manufacturing, Inc., Melrose Park, IL

10 9 8 7 6 5 4 3 2 1

To Our Readers
We have done our best to make sure all Internet Addresses in this book were active and appropriate when we went to press.
However, the author and the publisher have no control over and assume no liability for the material available on those Internet
sites or on other Web sites they may link to. Any comments or suggestions can be sent by e-mail to comments@enslow.com or
to the address on the back cover.

Every effort has been made to locate all copyright holders of material used in this book. If any errors or omissions have occurred,
corrections will be made in future editions of this book.

♻ Enslow Publishers, Inc., is committed to printing our books on recycled paper. The paper in every book contains 10% to
30% post-consumer waste (PCW). The cover board on the outside of each book contains 100% PCW. Our goal is to do our
part to help young people and the environment too!

Illustration Credits: Artville, p. 7; Associated Press, pp. 1 (lower right), 6, 23, 24; Bettmann/CORBIS, p. 26; Mary Evans Picture
Library/Everett Collection, p. 19; Advertising Archives/Courtesy Everett Collection, pp. 1 (upper left), 20, 29, 31; Granger Collection,
p. 9; Jeffrey Greenberg/Photo Researchers, p. 4; Photo courtesy of the W. K. Kellogg Foundation, p. 13; Library of Congress,
p. 14; Dennis MacDonald/Alamy, p. 27; Photos.com, p. 10; Shutterstock, pp. 3, 8, 11; Wikimedia Commons, p. 15.

Front Cover Illustrations: Associated Press (inset); Shutterstock (background).
Back Cover Illustration: Shutterstock.

Contents

For many years, kids have enjoyed the cereals from W. K. Kellogg's company.

Chapter 1

Destruction and Determination

He never ran for office. He never became president or mayor or starred in a movie. But everybody knows his name. Everybody has read it hundreds and hundreds of times. Maybe you saw it this morning on a box on your breakfast table.

Will Keith Kellogg, the "king of cornflakes," says good morning to the world in about 160 countries. That's more than most of us can find on a globe of the earth.

Flash back to the Fourth of July 1907. The sky was filled with a raging, roaring fire as Kellogg's breakfast-food factory burned down to the ground. Wisps of dark smoke curled around Kellogg's legs.

Will Keith Kellogg

Machinery was twisted into weird shapes. His brand-new factory had been shipping out thousands of boxes of cornflakes every day for just about one year. In one terrible night almost everything was blackened or broken.

Will Keith Kellogg, the forty-seven-year-old man who invented cornflakes, turned slowly to the crowd of workers shuffling through the smoke-filled mess. He shouted, "You will not be laid off. You can be used in construction and clean-up. Report here tomorrow morning!" Long into the night he made plans for new buildings. Quietly, forcefully, he borrowed money. He ordered new machinery. He started over, determined to succeed.

Chapter 2

"I Never Learned to Play"

Every one of us is different. We are not assembled in factories like dolls or robots. What happens to us as we grow up shapes us and changes us.

Will Kellogg had a very special kind of life. His father, John Preston Kellogg, married Mary Ann Call. She died early in the marriage, leaving her husband and two children. John Preston Kellogg married again. He and his second wife, Ann Janette Stanley, had a dozen more children. Will was born on April 7, 1860, in Battle Creek, Michigan. Being one of fourteen children is like living in a

small village under one roof. His hardworking mother even wove cloth and sewed it into clothing for every one of them.

The Kellogg family had little, but they gave generously. When a neighbor family needed a loom to weave cloth, Will's mother gave them hers. When another neighbor needed milk for his children, Will's

father gave him one of his two cows.

At this time, many people in the southern United States owned slaves. Many slaves ran away to live in Canada so they could be free. They traveled through free states, such as Michigan, where the Kelloggs lived. Some would knock on the Kelloggs' door in the

This painting shows people helping slaves escape in a system called the Underground Railroad. The Kellogg family helped slaves escape to freedom.

middle of the night. Will's dad would lead them to the next stop on the Underground Railroad so they would not be caught and sent back to their owners. The Underground Railroad was not a regular railroad with engines and tracks. It was a secret system of good people who hated slavery. They risked their lives and their homes to guide slaves to freedom in Canada.

To make a little bit of cash, the Kellogg kids grew vegetables, washed them, put them in bunches and sold them. There were no toys. There was not much time for play. There were no dogs to chase around. There was just an old horse called Spot

Like these children, the Kellogg kids grew vegetables in their garden to help feed the family.

that Will loved with all his heart.

Will's last year of school was sixth grade. He had trouble reading and writing because all the words were fuzzy. He desperately needed glasses. He was twenty before he got his first pair. Will never said it was a bad life. It was the one

given to him. Almost everything in his young life would shape all the rest of his days.

Chapter 3

The Super Salesman Sweeps Up

In 1867, seven-year-old Will started working in a broom factory his father set up. He rushed around bringing straw and broom handles to the workers. Then he learned how to make brooms himself. When Will was a teenager, his father put him in charge of the whole factory. At fifteen, he was sent on the road to sell brooms from one town to another across the Midwest.

On Will's very first day as a traveling salesman, there was a huge snowstorm. He loaded up his wagon. The horse bolted, throwing every broom into the snowdrifts. He loaded up the brooms again one by one. The wagon tipped over, throwing brooms all over the place. He loaded up again. It happened again. "If I didn't have so much pride I would have quit," he later declared. This boy was not a quitter.

Will always said he was bashful, but he turned out to be a natural salesman. At eighteen, he was offered a job managing a broom factory in faraway Dallas, Texas. His memory of those days was always sharp and clear. His boss was lazy. The man never paid his bills. Dallas was a rough, tough town. Will was lonely. He wrote in a letter home, "Had lots of company in the hotel last night. Bedbugs and fleas." He

At a young age, Will traveled across the Midwest selling brooms.

packed up, raced home to Battle Creek, and married his girlfriend, Ella Davis, on November 3, 1880.

Will signed up for courses at a business college. His headmaster promised, "You take this seat right

Dr. John Harvey Kellogg, Will Keith Kellogg's older brother

next to my desk. Work like hell. Anytime you want to know something, just say the word." In three months Will graduated as an accountant who knew how to keep business records. He went to work for his brother, Dr. John Harvey Kellogg.

His big brother was actually only five feet four inches tall. But he had a giant personality. The Seventh-Day Adventist Church, which the Kellogg family attended, had sent John to college to become a doctor. When he graduated, the church put him in charge of their famous sanitarium in Battle Creek. (A sanitarium is like a fancy clinic or health spa.) At twenty-four, John Kellogg was running a clinic known all around the world.

The sanitarium, known as the "San," featured water cures, hot and steamy or cold enough to cause goosebumps. The San included outdoor sunbaths in swimsuits on wintry days. People spent hours soaking up rays under huge panels of electric lights and endless hours exercising. There were tasteless meals with no meat and no alcohol. Absolutely no tobacco was allowed. It was very strict. But the rich and famous eagerly paid a fortune to stay there.

People at the sanitarium in Battle Creek doing breathing exercises. Exercise and proper diet were important at the San.

Chapter 4

The Billion-Dollar Mistake

Will Kellogg worked fifteen hours a day. He became the janitor, bookkeeper, and repairman, fixing all kinds of problems. He packed and shipped the books and medicines his brother sold all over the world. Every day you could see Dr. John Harvey Kellogg on a bicycle. Will would run alongside him with pad and pencil in his hands. He was taking down work orders. The doctor would pedal off for a pleasant ride while Will went to work. He kept on working like that at the clinic for twenty-five years. The whole arrangement between them was a mystery he never tried to explain.

Will Kellogg had almost no time for his two sons or for his wife, who was rather sickly. Doctor John Kellogg grew richer, while Will wrote in his diary, "I feel kind of blue. Am afraid I'll always be a poor man the way things look now." The doctor wrote more books and sold more health food through mail order. Will managed each business as it came along.

The brothers even made breakfast food from wheat. They cooked it, ran it through hot rollers, and watched the grains become flakes. It was healthy food, not fun food. It was not very tasty. But that is

How Cereal Is Made

Genius at Work!

- Grain—corn, rice, or wheat—arrives at the factory by the trainload to be inspected, cleaned, and weighed.

- Flavorings, vitamins, sweeteners, salt, and water are added to the grain.

- The mixture is cooked under steam pressure in giant cookers.

- The hot, wet mixture is dried with hot air, then cooled for several hours.

- Huge rollers flatten the cooked grain, turning it into flakes.

- The flakes are placed on a conveyor belt and moved to ovens where they are further dried and toasted, then bagged, boxed, and delivered to a store near you.

what the doctor ordered. Batch after batch was cooked up, packed up, and mailed out. Then one weekend there was a disaster.

A batch of wheat dough was left standing over Saturday and Sunday. Without refrigeration, it was ruined. Will ran the strange-tasting, strange-smelling stuff through hot rollers. The new flakes were interesting. He added sugar. The doctor did not want sugar. Will wanted to advertise the great new taste. John refused. The two brothers fought. They split up in 1906. They hardly ever spoke again.

Will Kellogg set up his own business—the Battle Creek Toasted Corn Flake Company. He started making cereal with whole-kernel corn. Then he switched to hominy grits, which are made of ground-up corn. He added some sugar. He said to his employees, "I'm not interested in a mail-order business. I want to sell those cornflakes by the carload!" His invention was ready to fly high.

In less than a year he was shipping forty-two hundred cases of cornflakes a day. He had a genius for advertising and the courage to spend $300,000 on full-page newspaper ads in 1907. One headline seemed crazy: "Please Stop Eating Corn Flakes for 30 Days … so we can catch up." It was such a wild idea that it worked miracles in sales. Then business almost stopped dead.

The Kellogg factory

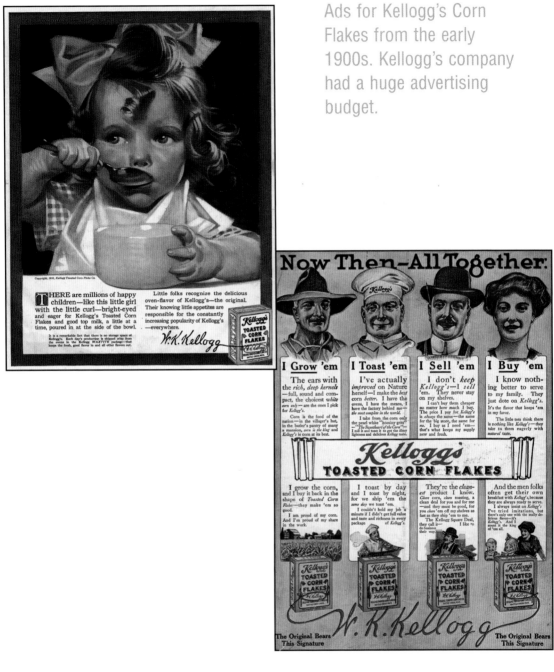

Ads for Kellogg's Corn Flakes from the early 1900s. Kellogg's company had a huge advertising budget.

The Great Depression hit hard in 1929. Jobs disappeared. Families lost their homes. Will Kellogg set up his factory with four six-hour job shifts each day, so more people could earn money in his plant. And then he sent out an order to double the advertising budget, saying, "Advertising pays!" By 1940 the Kellogg Company had spent $100 million on advertising.

The little brother who made a big mistake one weekend made a fortune faster than he could believe. His invention of cornflakes started bringing in billions of dollars a year.

Chapter 5

Investing in People

Will Kellogg had always lived a in a small house without a lot of money. Now he had tons of money flowing into his bank accounts. He started building a new life—a beautiful house on a lake in Michigan, another mansion in Florida, and a horse ranch in southern California.

He remembered that his childhood horse, old Spot, was a breed called an Arabian. So he bought ninety Arabians, which make exciting racehorses. He built grandstands for thousands of spectators to watch them race.

As a salesman he had loved traveling. Now he circled the world on steamships, railroads, and special cars with beds and baths and kitchens. His wife Ella had died in 1912, leaving two boys and a girl. In 1918 he married Dr. Carrie Staines, who had worked at the Battle Creek Sanitarium.

From the time he was a boy Kellogg had always wanted a dog. A couple of German shepherds became part of his life. His eyesight was failing, so they took care of him and he took care of them.

Kellogg built a beautiful house on Gull Lake in Michigan.

Kellogg raised beautiful Arabian horses.

Will Kellogg's secret joy was chocolate. The multimillionaire always had chocolate bars in his pocket. He also drank chocolate sodas when he could have afforded expensive champagne.

The real secret was that he paid off mortgages for people in Battle Creek who were in danger of losing their homes. He paid doctor's bills for people who never knew where the money came from. Finally he made his big move. He said, "I know how to invest my money. I'll invest it in people."

As the Great Depression rolled over people's lives, he put money into the W. K. Kellogg Foundation. It poured money into medical programs and small cities that needed help. In 1934 Will Keith Kellogg gave his foundation $66 million in Kellogg Company stock. Its value grew and grew until it reached almost $8 billion. "I want to see what you fellows are going to do while I'm still alive," he said to the people running his foundation. He watched

Will Kellogg with some members of his family: his wife, two of his daughters, and his sister Clara

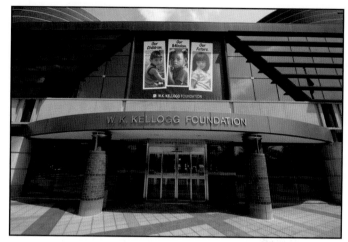

The headquarters of the W. K. Kellogg Foundation in Battle Creek. The money Kellogg made is still helping people today.

them carefully six days a week for twenty-one years. And then he died peacefully on October 6, 1951.

The bashful boy became a super salesman, a tireless inventor, a courageous advertiser, and a good friend to thousands of people who never got to meet him.

His fabulous investment in people goes on growing bigger and bigger. It is his way of saying "Good morning, world."

Timeline

1860 Born April 7, in Battle Creek, Michigan.

1867 Begins to work in father's broom factory.

1874 Becomes traveling salesman for father's broom factory.

1878 Takes job as manager of another broom factory in Dallas, Texas.

1880 Begins work at Battle Creek Sanitarium for his brother, Dr. John Harvey Kellogg.

Marries first wife, Ella Davis, November 3.

1894 Will and Dr. John Kellogg develop and sell wheat breakfast food through the mail. Wheat dough spoils when left out of refrigerator for two days. Will cooks it up into new version of wheat breakfast food.

1906 Brothers battle over business plans. They split apart. Will invents toasted cornflakes. He builds factory shipping thousands of cases a day.

1907 Cornflake factory burns down. Rebuilding starts immediately. Huge advertising campaigns sell thousands of cases Kellogg's Corn Flakes a day.

1912 Ella Kellogg dies, leaving three children.

1918   Marries Dr. Carrie Staines.

1925   Builds famous Arabian horse ranch in California.

1928   Adds Rice Krispies to the Kellogg lineup of cereals; more varieties follow.

1930   W. K. Kellogg Foundation starts giving money to medical research programs, schools, and small cities in Michigan and then in other states and countries.

1951   Dies October 6, one of the richest, most generous men in the world.

2005   W. K. Kellogg Foundation's seventy-fifth year. It is the seventh-largest charitable foundation in the United States, with $7.3 billion dollars at work.

Words to Know

foundation—An organization that manages money donated by a person or company. The foundation gives part of the money for good causes. Part of the money is invested so that there is more for future years.

hominy (HA-muh-nee) grits—A food made by soaking kernels of corn, removing the outer skin and grinding up the insides, then boiling them.

mortgage (MORE-gij)—A loan used to buy a house.

Seventh-day Adventists—Members of a Christian church that has strict rules against smoking, alcohol, and eating meat. They go to church on Saturday, not on Sunday.

sanitarium (san-ih-TARE-ee-um)—A health spa or clinic.

Underground Railroad—A secret system of people who helped slaves escape to Canada.

Books

Peterson, Tiffany. *W. K. Kellogg*. Chicago: Heinemann Library, 2003.

Slavin, Bill, with Jim Slavin. *Transformed: How Everyday Things Are Made*. Toronto: Kids Can Press, 2005.

St. George, Judith. *So You Want to Be an Inventor?* New York: Philomel Books, 2002.

Waxman, Laura Hamilton. *W. K. Kellogg*. Minneapolis: Lerner Publications, 2007.

"Now Ain't You Glad You Came?"

The very sight of Kellogg's Toasted Corn Flakes makes you want to grab a spoon and go to it.

ART CONTEST
$4,850.00 in Prizes for Pictures of Children

Artists, Amateurs and Art Students, send for book, "Childhood in Art," giving details of the Kellogg Prize Art Competition. 1st prize, $1,500; 2d prize, $1,000. 3d prize, $500; two 4th prizes, $250 each. Even if you have not won a prize, we will buy it if it has merit. The gentlemen who will serve as judges of the contest are A. W. Drake, Art Editor of the Century Magazine, Joseph H. Chapin, Art Editor of Scribner's, and Roy Brown, Art Editor of Everybody's Magazine.
In writing for book, address

THE KELLOGG PRIZE ART COMPETITION
381 Fourth Avenue   New York City

Everybody, child or grown-up, from two to toothless, feels the taste appeal of the famous Kellogg flavor.

Easy to serve—just three minutes from package to table, and this includes two minutes re-crisping in an open oven. Fresh always.

Kellogg's **TOASTED CORN FLAKES**

To prevent disappointment, don't merely ask for toasted corn flakes say "KELLOGG'S, please" and look for the signature on the package.

Web Sites

Kellogg's Company History
http://www.kellogghistory.com/

Inventor of the Week Archive: W. K. Kellogg
http://web.mit.edu/invent/iow/kellogg.html

Index